LIVING WELL

SAFETY FOR

BABYSITTERS

by Lucia Raatma

THE CHILD'S WORLD®
CHANHASSEN, MINNESOTA

The Child's World

Published in the United States of America by The Child's World®
PO Box 326, Chanhassen, MN 55317-0326
800-599-READ
www.childsworld.com

Subject Consultant:
Bridget Clementi,
Safe Kids Coordinator,
Children's Health
Education Center,
Milwaukee, Wisconsin

Photo Credits: Cover/frontispiece: BananaStock/Punchstock; cover corner: Comstock/Punchstock. Interior: Myrleen Ferguson Cate/PhotoEdit: 12, 22; Corbis: 5, 7, 10, 11 (LWA-Sharie Kennedy), 13 (Chuck Savage), 19, 23 (Jennie Woodcock; Reflections Photolibrary), 26 (Douglas Slone), 31 (John Henley); Mary Kate Denny/PhotoEdit: 9, 21; Getty Images/Photodisc: 8 (Mel Curtis), 15 (Ryan McVay), 16 (Amos Morgan), 17 (D. Falconer/PhotoLink); Getty Images/Stone/Nick Dolding: 18; Novastock/Stock Connection/PictureQuest: 6; PhotoEdit: 14 (Lon C. Diehl), 24 (Mary Steinbacher), 25 (Bill Aron), 27 (Michael Newman).

The Child's World®: Mary Berendes, Publishing Director

Editorial Directions, Inc.: E. Russell Primm, Editorial Director; Katie Marsico, Line Editor; Matt Messbarger, Editorial Assistant; Susan Hindman, Copy Editor; Sarah E. De Capua, Proofreader; Katherine Trickle and Stephen Carl Wender, Fact Checkers; Tim Griffin/IndexServ, Indexer; Cian Loughlin O'Day, Photo Researcher; Linda S. Koutris, Photo Selector

The Design Lab: Kathleen Petelinsek, Design; Kari Thornborough, Page Production

Library of Congress Cataloging-in-Publication Data
Raatma, Lucia.
   Safety for babysitters / by Lucia Raatma.
      v. cm. — (Living well (series))
   Includes bibliographical references and index.
   Contents: An evening at the Martins' house—Getting ready to babysit—Being in charge—How to have fun and be safe—What to do in an emergency—When the parents come home—Glossary—Questions and answers about babysitting safety—Helping a friend learn about babysitting safety—Did you know?—How to learn more about babysitting safety.
   ISBN 1-59296-239-4 (library bound : alk. paper)
   1. Babysitting—Vocational guidance—United States—Juvenile literature. [1. Babysitting—Handbooks, manuals, etc. 2. Safety.] I. Title. II. Living well (Child's World (Firm))
  HQ769.5.R22 2005
  649'.1'0248—dc22   2003027213

TABLE OF CONTENTS

CHAPTER ONE

AN EVENING AT THE MARTINS' HOUSE

"Jessica is here," called Mrs. Martin to her children. "Yeah!" Nicholas yelled as he hurried into the kitchen. "This will be fun," Anna squealed as she ran to give Jessica a hug. "What games will we play tonight?"

"Lots," Jessica answered. "But first things first. Mrs. Martin, any special instructions?" Jessica got out a pad and pen, and she listened as Mrs. Martin spoke.

"Well, Mr. Martin and I will be at Fredo's Restaurant. The phone number there is 555-7557. Nicholas and Anna have had dinner, but they can have a healthy snack before bed. Bedtime is 9 o'clock. We should be back by 11 o'clock," Mrs. Martin explained. "And you have been here so often before, you know where everything is."

Jessica listened and wrote down the name of the restaurant and the phone number. She also wrote "bedtime—9:00."

"Sounds great," Jessica said.

Mr. Martin came into the kitchen and said hello. Then he and his wife put on their coats and started out the back door.

"Be sure to lock up

When you babysit, remember to write down any special instructions the parents give you.

behind us," Mr. Martin said as he started to close the door.

"Yes, sir," Jessica replied. "Have fun and don't worry about a thing."

The door closed, and Jessica locked it. She turned on the outside light. Then she clapped her hands and faced Nicholas and Anna. "Who wants to pick the first game?"

Babysitting is a good way to earn money. But babysitters have a big **responsibility.** Parents trust them to take care of children and to keep them safe. By following a few rules, babysitters can be safe and have fun, too.

Babysitting is a fun way to earn money, but it is also a responsibility that must be taken seriously.

CHAPTER TWO

GETTING READY
TO BABYSIT

Have you ever watched your younger brother or sister when your

parents weren't home? Or have you ever helped out neighbors with

their younger kids? If so, you might be interested in babysitting.

But remember, babysitting is more than just playing games or

*Spending time with kids before you babysit is a good way
to tell if babysitting is the right job for you.*

It is helpful to have some experience with children before you accept an offer to babysit.

watching TV. Being a babysitter means that you are completely responsible for the children in your care.

If you have not spent much time around younger kids, you should get some experience first. Offer to spend the day with neighbors or other friends with young children. Help make lunch or watch the kids as they play.

You could also take a babysitting class. Many groups, such as the Girl Scouts or the Red Cross, offer these classes. In addition,

If you are considering becoming a babysitter, check with your local Girl Scout troop to see if they offer any babysitting classes.

it's a great idea to take classes in first aid.

Once you are ready to babysit, let people know. Tell your friends and neighbors. Most people find babysitters by word of mouth. They feel better if they know their babysitter's parents

An Imaginary Fire Drill

Walk through the home where you are babysitting, and imagine what you would do if there was a fire. Before parents leave, ask them if they have a fire extinguisher and where they keep it. Notice where all the windows and doors are located. They may be good ways out of a burning building. If you are in an apartment, see where the fire escape is. And never use an elevator during a fire. Plan an **escape route**. In the event of a fire, you should feel the door with the palm of your hand before opening it. If the door is hot, keep it shut and find another way out. Also remember that smoke rises, so you want to stay as close to the floor as you can. It is important to get out of the home as quickly as possible. Once you are out of the home, you should stay out. You can call 9-1-1 from a neighbor's house or from a cell phone.

or friends. And it is good for you to know who you are babysitting for. Personal **recommendations** make everyone feel safer.

Talk to the parents about your fee. Also discuss any extra jobs you will be expected to do while you babysit. These may include giving the kids a bath or doing household chores.

CHAPTER THREE

BEING IN CHARGE

Before the parents leave, ask about bedtimes. Find out what food

the kids can have. Ask about any medicine they need to take. Talk

to the parents about any dangers in the home. These may include

Always check with parents to see what snacks the kids are allowed to eat.

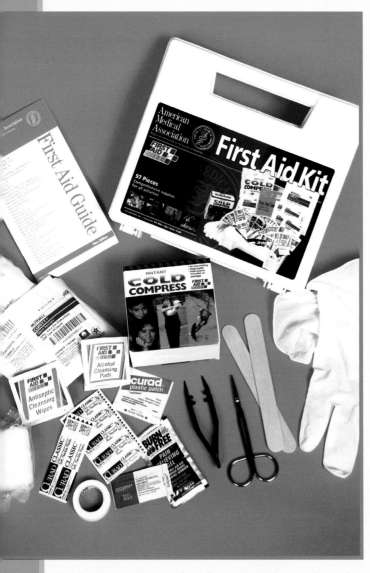

Make sure you know where first-aid supplies are located in the home so you can act quickly if an accident occurs.

guns, which should be locked up and kept out of reach. Matches and lighters should also be kept out of sight.

Ask about first-aid supplies. You should know where the bandages and **ointments** are kept. If you are babysitting for infants, be sure you know where the diapers are and how to change them. Be sure you know where to throw out dirty diapers.

Take time to talk to the children while their parents are still home. Let them get used to the idea that you are there. Also spend a few minutes meeting or greeting any family pets.

Even though you've been hired to watch the kids, you'll feel more comfortable if you also become familiar with family pets.

Be sure you know where the parents will be and how they can be reached. Also ask what time they expect to return. As the parents leave, lock the door behind them.

Then walk through the house and make sure all windows and doors are locked. If you are babysitting in the evening, turn on the outside lights, even if it is not dark yet. If there is a pool, make sure that the door or gate leading to it is locked.

If you answer the phone while you are babysitting,

Don't forget to lock the doors and windows after parents leave the house.

Be sure to turn on all outside lights if you babysit at night.

never say that the parents are out. Instead, say they cannot come

to the phone and offer to take a message.

Never open the door to a stranger while you are babysitting.

And if you take the children outside, do not talk to strangers.

CHAPTER FOUR

WHAT TO DO IN AN EMERGENCY

In case of an **emergency,** do not panic. Remember to stay calm and to think things through.

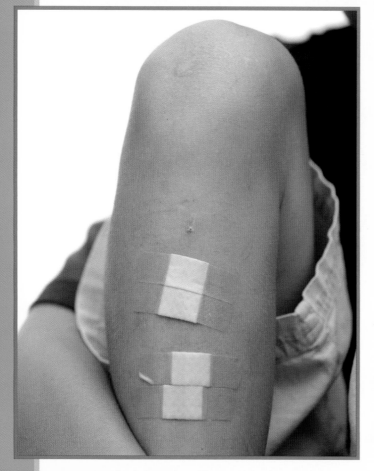

You might feel comfortable handling an accident such as a skinned knee, but you may need help if an injury is more serious.

If someone gets hurt, decide whether or not you can handle the problem. A skinned knee might only require a bandage and some antibacterial ointment. But a head injury, a broken bone, or difficulty breathing are examples of more

If you have to call 9-1-1 during an emergency, try to speak calmly and clearly. The operator will probably stay on the phone with you until help arrives.

serious situations. With those sorts of **accidents,** call the

parents at the number they have left for you. They will probably

return home to take care of the child. If you cannot reach them,

call 9-1-1 and listen to the operator's instructions.

If there is immediate danger, you must act quickly. In case of fire, get out of the house and make sure you take everyone with you. Once outside, call 9-1-1 and remain outside.

If someone tries to break in while you're babysitting, never try to confront that person. Instead, gather the children, find a safe place, and call 9-1-1.

If you think that someone is trying to break into the home, get everyone into a room, lock the door, and call 9-1-1. Or get out of the home and go to a neighbor's house. Don't try to be a hero. Your main goal is to keep yourself and the children you are watching safe from any harm.

A Babysitter's Checklist

Before the parents leave, always get answers to the following questions:

1. Where will the parents be? What phone number can you use to reach them? In case you can't reach the parents, who else can be contacted in an emergency?

2. When will the parents return?

3. Are the matches and lighters stored out of reach? How about insect sprays, cleaners, and medicines?

4. Where are first-aid supplies kept?

5. In case of fire, is there a fire escape or a second exit? Is there a fire extinguisher?

6. If you are babysitting at night, when is the children's bedtime?

7. What foods are the children allowed to eat? Do any of the children have food allergies? Are there any special instructions about health issues? Do any of the children need to be given medicine?

8. Are there any limits on watching TV, playing video games, or using the computer?

9. Depending on the time of day, are the children allowed to have friends over?

10. Should you answer the phone or just let the answering machine pick up?

CHAPTER FIVE

HOW TO HAVE
FUN AND BE SAFE

Kids will ask their parents to have you babysit over and over if

you are fun. Parents will keep hiring you if you are safe. So find

ways to be both fun and safe!

When you play with the kids you babysit for, they will love

it. But remember that the rules of the house should still be

followed. Make sure you know what those rules are.

That means no jumping on beds and no playing ball in the

house. But you can play hide-and-seek or a board game. You can

watch a kid-friendly movie or read together.

If you make a snack or meal, be sure to clean up the kitchen.

Never leave the oven or stove on, and make sure kids keep their

hands away from hot places. Also make sure knives and other

*Babysitting should be fun, but you need to follow the rules
of the house and see to it that everyone stays safe.*

sharp objects are out of their reach.

It is important to keep an eye on electric cords and **outlets**— especially when watching small children. Make

Don't forget to clean up if you make a snack for yourself or the kids.

sure kids do not pull on the cords or stick fingers, forks, or other

items into the outlets. Also, keep kids away from household

cleaners. These contain **chemicals** that could hurt them.

If you give the children a bath, never leave them alone, even

for a moment. Even just a few inches of water can be dangerous for them. Be sure to test the water before the kids get in the tub. Water that is too hot could cause a burn. Be sure to help them in and out of the bathtub.

After the kids are in bed, check on them every 15 or 20 minutes. You can watch TV quietly or read until the parents come home. Unless you have the

Make sure that kids aren't able to get to cleaning supplies or other products that might contain dangerous chemicals.

Even when the kids are sleeping, a babysitter's job still isn't over. It's important to check on the kids every so often until the parents return.

parents' permission, do not invite your friends over. And don't

talk on the phone for long periods of time. Remember you are

working, and babysitting is an important job.

CHAPTER SIX

WHEN THE PARENTS COME HOME

Once the parents return, make them aware of any problems

or concerns you had while they were away. Let them know

what their children ate and when they went to sleep. Also tell

Be open with parents about any problems you had while they were away.
If things went smoothly and you had a good time, tell them that, too!

If you feel uncomfortable about accepting a ride home from one of the parents, arrange for your own parents or another trusted adult to pick you up instead.

them about any phone messages you took. If you received any strange phone calls, give the parents those details.

If one of the parents offers to drive you home, make sure you feel safe about that. If you suspect they have been drinking or if you feel uncomfortable in any way, call your parents and ask them to pick you up.

Let the parents know if everything went well and tell them if you are eager to babysit again. No doubt they will appreciate the offer. They will like being able to count on you.

Even though babysitting is a huge responsibility, it can also be a rewarding experience for both you and the family you are working with.

Glossary

accidents (AK-si-duhntz) Accidents are events that take place unexpectedly and often involve people being injured.

chemicals (KEM-uh-kuhlz) Chemicals are substances used in household cleaners and other items. Some chemicals are dangerous.

emergency (i-MUR-juhn-see) An emergency is a sudden and dangerous situation that requires immediate attention.

escape route (ess-KAPE ROOT) An escape route is a planned way to leave a building in case of an emergency.

first aid (FURST AYD) First aid is immediate care given to an injured or sick person.

ointments (OYNT-ments) Ointments are medicines to put on burns and scrapes.

outlets (OUT-lets) Outlets are places where appliances and other machines can be plugged in to receive electricity.

recommendations (rek-uh-mend-AY-shunz) Recommendations are suggestions for something or someone good. People give recommendations when they believe another person is well suited for a job.

responsibility (ri-spon-suh-BIL-uh-tee) A responsibility is a duty or a job.

Questions and Answers about Babysitting Safety

Babysitting is easy. All you do is watch TV while the kids sleep, right? No! You might get a chance to relax, but don't count on it. Most of your time will be spent taking care of the children and keeping them safe. It is a big responsibility.

When do I know to call 9-1-1? You will know it is an emergency if you can't solve the problem on your own and if you don't have time for the parents to return home. Examples of this type of situation are a fire or an attempted break-in.

Is it OK to help myself to snacks? Maybe. Ask the parents first. Most will tell you to enjoy a snack while you are babysitting, but certain foods may be off-limits.

The kids say their parents always let them stay up late on weekends. Should I believe them? Don't put yourself in that situation. Always confirm the bedtime before the parents leave.

Helping a Friend Learn about Babysitting Safety

▸ Offer to take a babysitting class with a friend. The two of you may enjoy attending the class together, and you can help each other learn the rules.

▸ With the parents' permission, have a friend help you babysit. This way, she can see what you do and get hands-on experience.

▸ Review the checklist (on page 19) with your friend. You both can talk about why each question is important.

Did You Know?

▸ It is always best to know the people you are babysitting for. If someone you regularly babysit for recommends you to strangers, get together with these new people beforehand or spend some time talking with them on the phone. This will help you get to know them a little better and will probably make it more comfortable for you when it comes time to babysit.

▸ If you do not know the children well, it might be best to schedule a visit before you babysit. This way, you can become more familiar with the kids and their home.

▸ It is a good idea to check with your parents before taking a babysitting job. Tell them the date and time. And be sure to leave them the name, address, and phone number of the family you are babysitting for.

How to Learn More about Babysitting Safety

At the Library

Brown, Harriet. *The Babysitter's Handbook: The Care and Keeping of Kids.* Middleton, Wis.: Pleasant Company, 1999.

Fine, Jil. *Babysitting Smarts.* Danbury, Conn.: Children's Press, 2002.

Kuch, K. D. *The Babysitter's Handbook.* New York: Random House, 1997.

On the Web

Visit our home page for lots of links about babysitting safety:
http://www.childsworld.com/links.html

Note to Parents, Teachers, and Librarians: We routinely verify our Web links to make sure they're safe, active sites—so encourage your readers to check them out!

Through the Mail or by Phone

American Red Cross National Headquarters
431 18th Street NW
Washington, DC 20006
202/303-4498

National SAFE KIDS Campaign
1301 Pennsylvania Avenue NW
Suite 100
Washington, DC 20004
202/662-0600

Safe Sitter, Inc.
5670 Caito Drive,
Suite 172
Indianapolis, IN 46226
317/543-3840

Index

About the Author

Lucia Raatma received her bachelor's degree in English literature from the University of South Carolina and her master's degree in cinema studies from New York University. She has written a wide range of books for young people. When she is not researching or writing, she enjoys going to movies, practicing yoga, and spending time with her family. She lives in New York.